Can Read Music

A NOTE SPELLER FOR PIANO

By Nancy and Randall Faber

Contents

Special thanks and acknowledgement to
Crystal Bowman and Jennifer McLean
for the StoryRhymes.

Production: Frank and Gail Hackinson
Production Coordinator: Marilyn Cole
Cover and illustrations: Gwen Terpstra Design, San Francisco
Music Editor: Edwin McLean
Engraving: GrayBear Music Company, Hollywood, Florida
Printer: Trend Graphics

Lesson 1   Guide Note Review

These color illustrations can help you remember the seven "guide notes" introduced in *I Can Read Music* Book One.

The first letter of each word gives the note name.

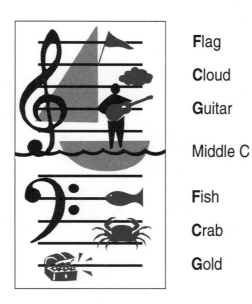

Flag

Cloud

Guitar

Middle C

Fish

Crab

Gold

Name each guide note in the boxes to the right.

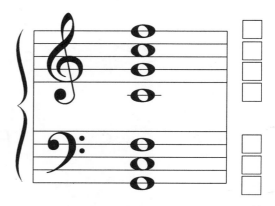

Now play these seven guide notes on the keyboard going *up* the staff, then coming *down* the staff.

Circle every C.

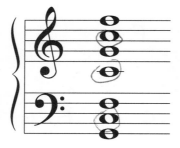

Circle every G.

Circle every F.

Write the letter names for the following guide notes. Notice the clef signs! Then play each note on the keyboard.

G

F

C

G

C

G

F

C

The Greatest Gadget

Words by Jennifer McLean

Guide Notes

This *StoryRhyme* uses the seven guide notes you have learned.
Name each note to complete the *StoryRhyme*.

My unCle Gave me a G ad G et

that does Countless Crazy things.

It Gan CatCh a Fish and Fry one,

or Cook FlapjaC ks fit for kinGs.

It Can be a GrapeFruit peeler, a Fork or spoon or kniFe.

It's the niF tiest of G ad G ets I've seen in all my liFe.

It's even learned to mow the yard and sCrub the kitChen Floor.

Now I have more time to play beCause it does my Chores.

We love this Funny "thinGy" but my story's Far from over.

We just Can't seem to turn it oFF and now it's Chasin G Rover!

(Your teacher may ask you to play the notes in the *StoryRhyme* on the piano.)

Lesson 2   Intervals — 2nds and 3rds

An *interval* is the distance between two notes on the staff or two keys on the keyboard.

2nd = step
(second)

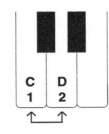

A **2nd** is:

   or

a line to a space   **a space to a line**

Draw a 2nd *above* each of the following guide notes. Then name both notes in the blanks.

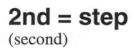 Ex. G A

 C D

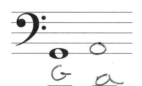 G a

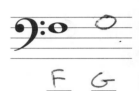 F G

Draw a 2nd *below* each of the following guide notes. Then name both notes in the blanks.

 G F

 C B

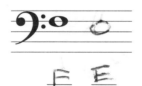 F E

 F E

3rd = skip
(third)

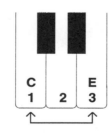

A **3rd** is:

   or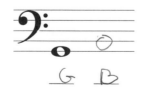

a line to a line   **a space to a space**

Draw a 3rd *above* each of the following guide notes. Then name both notes in the blanks.

 C E

 C E

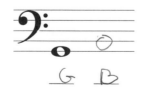 G B

 G B

Draw a 3rd *below* each of the following guide notes. Then name both notes in the blanks.

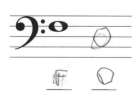 F D

 F D

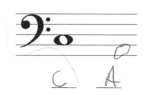 C A

 C A

Extra Credit: Your teacher may ask you to play all the examples above on the keyboard.

Sightreading Bonanza!

Dear Student: These short examples will help make you a "pro" at reading music. Each example begins on a guide note you have learned. Your teacher will ask you to sightread this page and will help keep a record of your progress with "Bull's-eyes" and "Misses."

Bull's-eye = correct note   **Miss = incorrect note or rhythm**

Teacher's Note: Record the number of incorrect notes and rhythms under "Misses." For "Bull's-eyes," subtract the number of "Misses" from the Perfect score (50) given at the bottom of the page.

Sightreading Tips: 1. **Set a steady beat by counting one "free" measure.**
2. **Keep your eyes on the music.**
3. **Play rather slowly always moving your eyes ahead.**
4. **Keep going no matter what!**

Do this page with your teacher each week and write down your score.

See if you can get your "Misses" down to zero by the third week!

Perfect score: 50

Date: **Score:**

_____ (1st week)   _____ Bull's-eyes   _____ Misses

_____ (2nd week)   _____ Bull's-eyes   _____ Misses

_____ (3rd week)   _____ Bull's-eyes   _____ Misses

Lesson 3 — Treble Space Notes

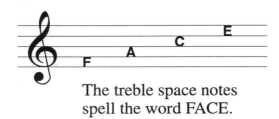

The treble space notes spell the word FACE.

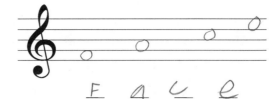

F A C E

Draw a whole note in each space, then name each note in the blank.

1. Which space note is a "guide note" you have already learned? _____

2. Play each of these space notes on the keyboard saying the note names aloud. Remember to start on the first F above Middle C.

3. Are the space notes a **2nd** or a **3rd** apart? _____

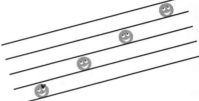

Faces in the Spaces

Using whole notes, draw the following space notes on the treble staff. Then play each example on the keyboard.

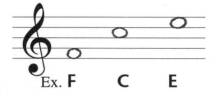
Ex. F   C   E

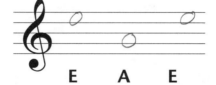
E   A   E

A   F   E

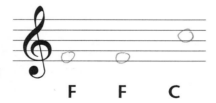
F   F   C

C   E   A

E   C   F

Name each note used in the 3rds below. Then play each 3rd on the keyboard. Use fingers 1 and 3, or 2 and 4.

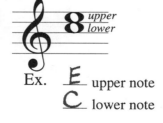
Ex. E upper note
    C lower note

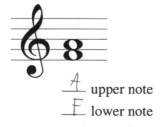
A upper note
F lower note

C upper note
A lower note

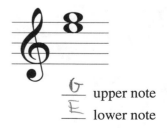
G upper note
E lower note

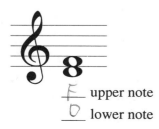
F upper note
D lower note

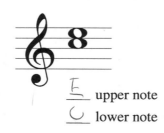
E upper note
C lower note

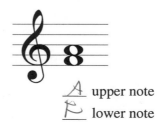
A upper note
F lower note

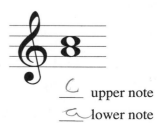
C upper note
A lower note

FF

Two More Treble Space Notes

Find the D and G treble space notes on the piano. Say the letter names aloud.

Loading the Spaceship

This spaceship is beaming up its cargo (space notes).

Draw a line connecting each space note to the correct part of the spaceship (correct key).

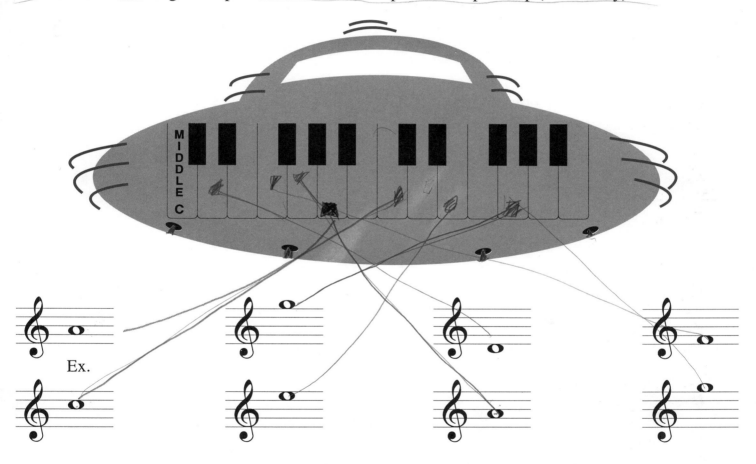

Ex.

Circle the correct music for the letter names below. Then play the circled examples on the piano.

F A C E or   **D F A G** or   **F E A G** or

Heebee Jeebees

Words by Crystal Bowman

This *StoryRhyme* uses the six treble space notes you have learned.

Please don't scrAtch the ChAlkboArd, I just Don't likE that sound.

It Gives me heebee jeebees and my skin CrAwls up and Down.

When you eat your ____inner, please don't s__r__p__ your pl__t__.

I get the heebee jeebees when I hear those sounds I hate!

The heebee jeebees get me when I s____ : things I ___r__ ___ ___.

Like roaches in the ____los__t, and spiders in my b__ ___.

I get the h____bee jeebees, I shiver, sh__k__ and squirm,

when ___ ___ p inside an ___pple, I ___in ___ a tiny worm.

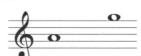 

Listen to me, ___hil___r___n, this w___rnin___ is for you.

Be ___ ___r ___ful what you see and h___ ___r, or they may ___ ___t you, too!

(Your teacher may ask you to play the notes in the *StoryRhyme* on the piano.)

10-1

Sightreading Bonanza!

Sightread these musical examples for the R.H. Each one begins on a **treble space note** and uses 2nds and 3rds.

Your teacher will keep a record of your progress with "Wonderful Notes" (correct notes) and "Wacky Notes" (incorrect notes).

1.

2.

3.

4.

5.

Do this page with your teacher each week and write down your score.

See how close you can get to the "wonderful" score of 50 by the third week!

Perfect score: 50

Date: **Score:**

_____ (1st week)   _____50_____ **Wonderful Notes**   ___42___ **Wacky Notes**

_____ (2nd week)   _____ **Wonderful Notes**   _____ **Wacky Notes**

_____ (3rd week)   _____ **Wonderful Notes**   _____ **Wacky Notes**

Lesson 4

Bass Space Notes

2-25

The word "FACE" can also help you learn the *bass* space notes.
Be careful, though, because in the bass clef, the F is *below* the staff:

(2nd F below Middle C)

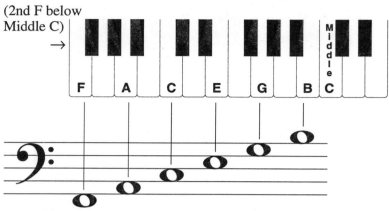

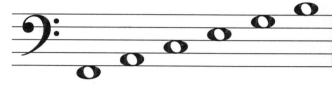

Play each of these space notes going up
and going down the keyboard.
Say the letter names aloud as you play.

Name the space notes in the blanks above.

Face the Bass

Write the name of each space note in the blank.
Then play each note on the keyboard.

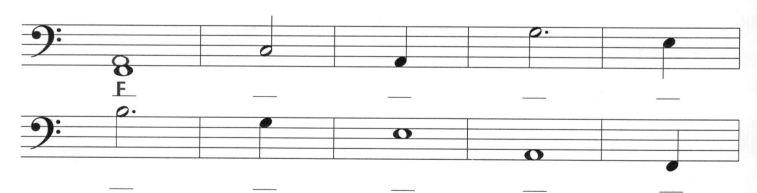

Using **only bass space notes**, draw whole notes for the letter names below.

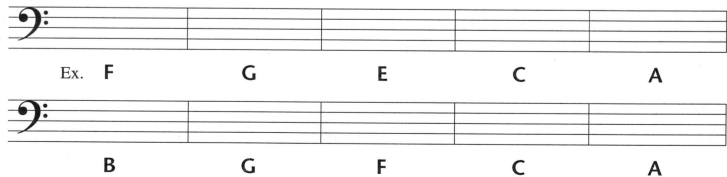

| Ex. F | G | E | C | A |

| B | G | F | C | A |

(Your teacher may ask you to play each note you have written on the piano.)

10

FF

Space Travel on the Grand Staff

Remember, the space notes move up and down the grand staff in 3rds.
Write the correct letter name for each space note below.

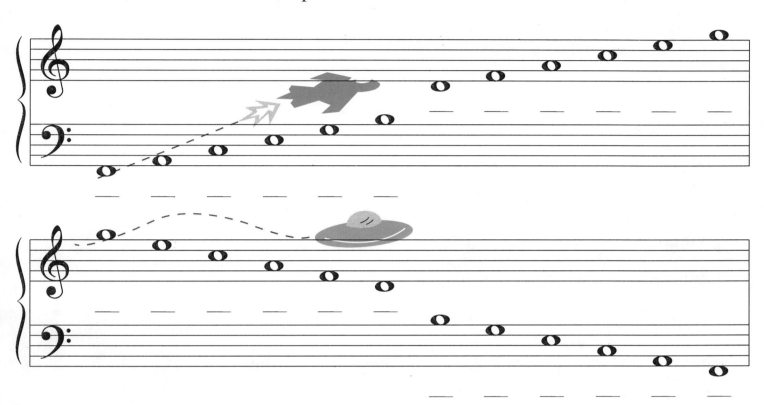

Reviewing 2nds and 3rds

Write the correct interval from each space note given below. Then name both notes.
Your teacher may ask you to play them on the piano.

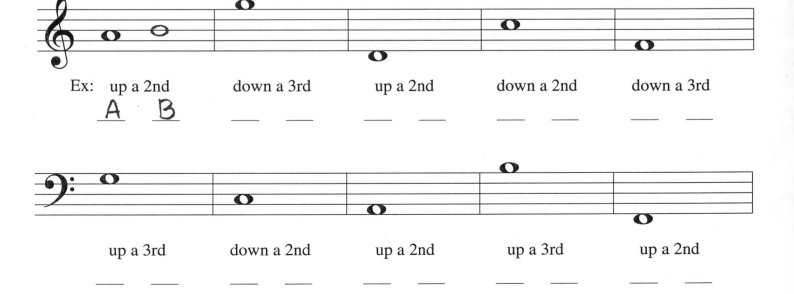

Ex: up a 2nd   down a 3rd   up a 2nd   down a 2nd   down a 3rd

A B

up a 3rd   down a 2nd   up a 2nd   up a 3rd   up a 2nd

Bug in My Stew

Words by Crystal Bowman

This *StoryRhyme* uses all the space notes of the grand staff (treble and bass staffs together).
Be sure to notice the clef signs!

I was ___tin___ my st__w then ___ ___i ___ to stop,

be___use a ___u___ was ___lo___tin___ right there on the top.

I didn't ___ ___t fri___ht___n___d or let out a shout,

I simply decided to get the bug out.

The st__w was ___ ___li___ious, I have to ___dmit,

It t__st__d so good that I ___te quite a ___it.

I ___ ___in ___lly ___ ___inished and there in my mu__ ,

way at the ___ottom I s__w one more ___u__ .

I ___ oul___ have been ___ n___ry, I could have ___ ___ ___n sad,

But the st__w was the ___ ___st that I ever h___ ___.

So when you are making a flavorful stew, remember to throw in a small bug or two! *Just kidding!*

(Your teacher may ask you to play the notes in the *StoryRhyme* on the piano.)

Sightreading Bonanza!

Sightread these musical examples for the L.H. Each one begins on a bass space note and uses 2nds and 3rds. Remember to set one full measure of a slow, steady tempo before you begin.

Your teacher will keep a record of your progress with "Great Notes" (correct notes) and "Grumpy Notes" (incorrect notes).

1.

2.

3.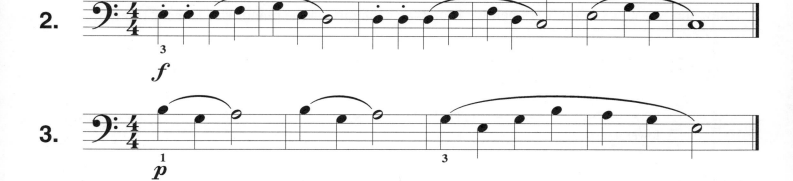

4.

5.

Do this page with your teacher each week and write down your score.

Perfect score: 50

Date: **Score:**

_____ (1st week)   _____ **Great Notes**   _____ **Grumpy Notes**

_____ (2nd week)   _____ **Great Notes**   _____ **Grumpy Notes**

_____ (3rd week)   _____ **Great Notes**   _____ **Grumpy Notes**

Lesson 5

The 5th (Fifth)

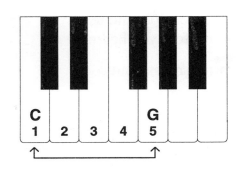

A **5th** is
a space to a space

or

a line to a line.

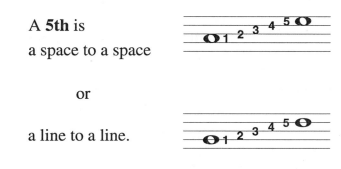

Think of a 5th as a "double skip."

5ths on Spaces

Name the two notes in each 5th below. Then play each one on the piano. Use fingers 1 and 5.

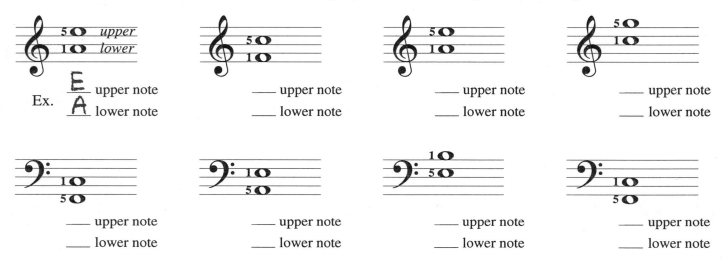

Ex.
____ **E** upper note
____ **A** lower note

____ upper note
____ lower note

____ upper note
____ lower note

____ upper note
____ lower note

____ upper note
____ lower note

____ upper note
____ lower note

____ upper note
____ lower note

____ upper note
____ lower note

5ths on Lines

Circle the correct letter names for each 5th. Then play these 5ths on the keyboard.

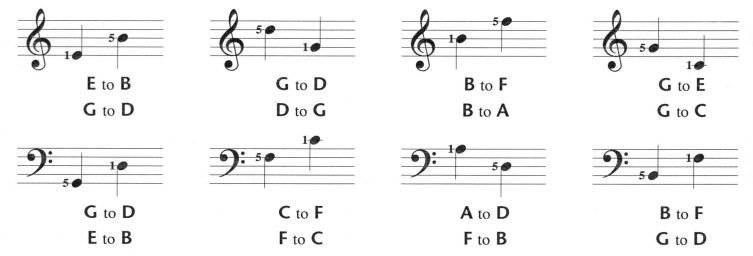

E to B
G to D

G to D
D to G

B to F
B to A

G to E
G to C

G to D
E to B

C to F
F to C

A to D
F to B

B to F
G to D

FF10

Finding 5ths

Find and circle each 5th in the examples below.

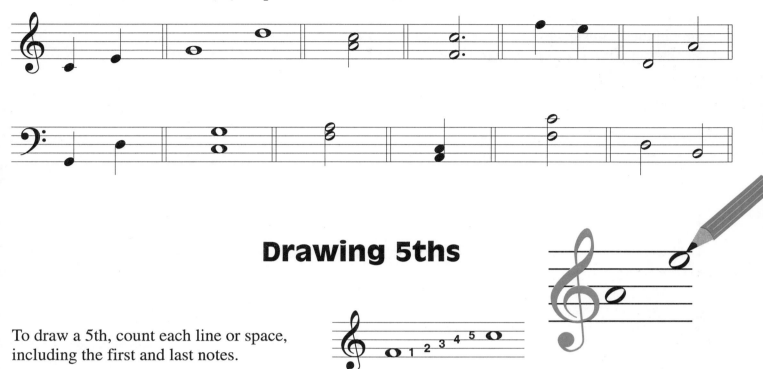

Drawing 5ths

To draw a 5th, count each line or space, including the first and last notes.

Draw a 5th above or below each given note. Use whole notes. Remember, a 5th is a "double skip." Then name both notes in the blanks. (Your teacher may ask you to play them on the piano.)

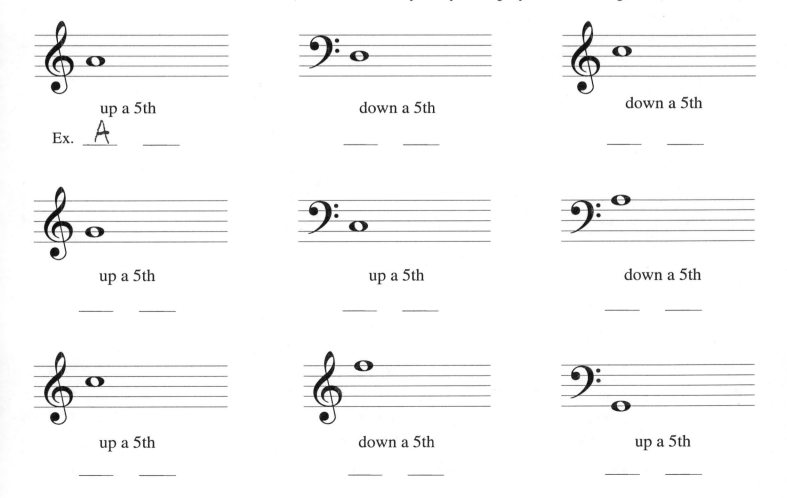

up a 5th

Ex. _A_ ____

down a 5th

____ ____

down a 5th

____ ____

up a 5th

____ ____

up a 5th

____ ____

down a 5th

____ ____

up a 5th

____ ____

down a 5th

____ ____

up a 5th

____ ____

Sightreading Bonanza!

Sightread these musical examples. Each one uses 5ths.
After finding your position, remember to set a slow, steady beat before you begin.

You teacher will keep a record of your progress with "Clever Notes" (correct notes) and
"Clunky Notes" (incorrect notes).

1.

2.

3.

4.

5.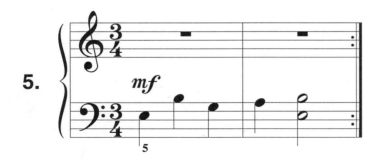

6.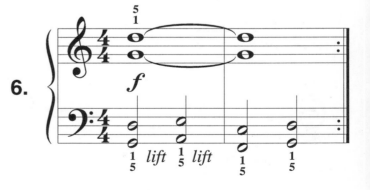

Do this page with your teacher each week and write down your score.

Perfect score: 50

Date: **Score:**

_____ (1st week)   _____ Clever Notes   _____ Clunky Notes

_____ (2nd week)   _____ Clever Notes   _____ Clunky Notes

_____ (3rd week)   _____ Clever Notes   _____ Clunky Notes

Lesson 6

The 4th (Fourth)

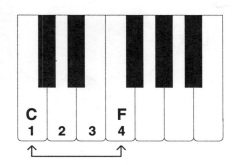

To write a 4th, count each line and space including the first and last notes.

A **4th** is:

a line to a space

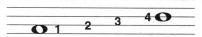

or

a space to a line.

Find and circle each 4th in the examples below.

Write 4ths *up* or *down* from the notes below. Then name both notes in the blanks.
When you are done, play each 4th on the piano. Notice the fingering!

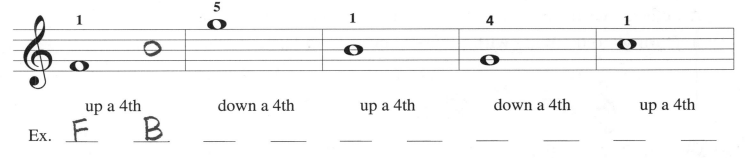

up a 4th   down a 4th   up a 4th   down a 4th   up a 4th

Ex. F   B   ___ ___   ___ ___   ___ ___   ___ ___

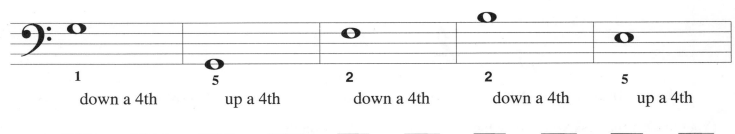

down a 4th   up a 4th   down a 4th   down a 4th   up a 4th

___ ___   ___ ___   ___ ___   ___ ___   ___ ___

Grandfather's Barn

Words by Jennifer McLean

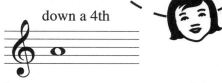

Draw the note that is a **4th** up or down from the note given.
Name both notes in the blanks and enjoy reading the *StoryRhyme!*

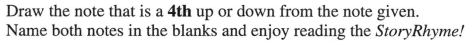

I love to visit my gr__n __ father's farm, bec __ us __ next to his

house is an old red barn. In it are lots of treasures to see,

like a __ o __ art __ n __ __ icycl __ waiting for me.

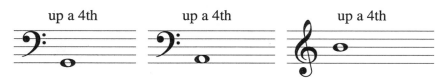

Under a __ __ dspre __ __ one __ __ y I found

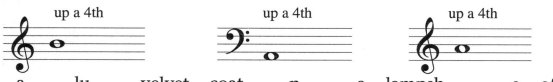

a __ lu __ velvet coat __ n __ a lampsh __ __ e of brown.

A clock with a co__w__b that covers its __ a __ e,
a funny old hat with some beads and white lace.

There's a br__n __ new __ __ venture __ __ hind the barn door,

for there's always a tr __ __ sure that I've missed __ e __ ore.

(Your teacher may ask you to play the 4ths in the *StoryRhyme* on the piano.)

18

FF1

Sightreading Bonanza!

Sightread these musical examples that use 4ths.

Hint: Before playing, take a moment to look over the music and locate the 4ths.
    Set a steady tempo of one full measure before you begin.

Your teacher will keep a record of your progress with "Smart Notes" (correct notes) and "Slip-ups" (incorrect notes).

Each week try to get closer to a perfect score!

1.
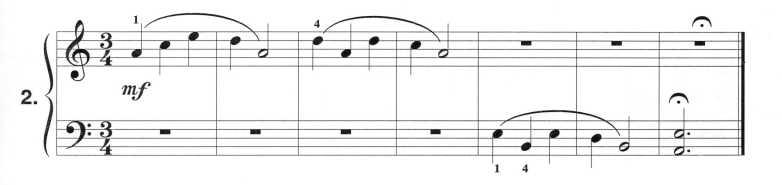

2.
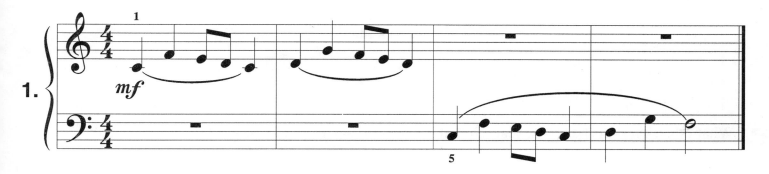

3.
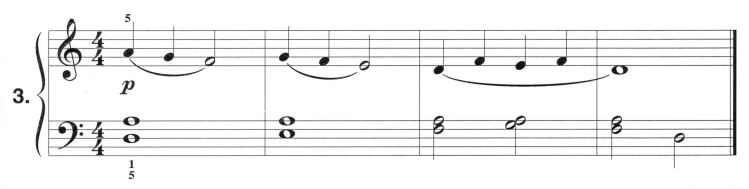

Perfect score: 50

Date: **Score:**

_____ (1st week)   _____ **Smart Notes**   _____ **Slip-ups**

_____ (2nd week)   _____ **Smart Notes**   _____ **Slip-ups**

_____ (3rd week)   _____ **Smart Notes**   _____ **Slip-ups**

The 6th (Sixth)

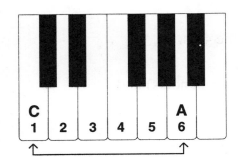

A **6th** is:

a line to a space

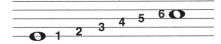

or

a space to a line.

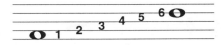

What other intervals have you learned that move from **a line to a space?**

2nd, 3rd, 4th, 5th

(circle two)

Name the notes below. Then play the 6ths on the keyboard.

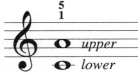

Ex.
$\frac{A}{C}$ upper note
lower note

—— upper note
—— lower note

—— upper note
—— lower note

—— upper note
—— lower note

—— upper note
—— lower note

—— upper note
—— lower note

—— upper note
—— lower note

—— upper note
—— lower note

Find and circle each 6th in the examples below.

Sixth Sense

Put a ✓ next to the correct interval names. Give yourself 5 points for each correct answer.

5th – 2nd ——
or
6th – 2nd ——

4th – 3rd ——
or
2nd – 3rd ——

6th – 5th ——
or
6th – 3rd ——

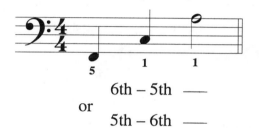

6th – 5th ——
or
5th – 6th ——

3rd – 6th ——
or
4th – 5th ——

4th – 5th ——
or
4th – 6th ——

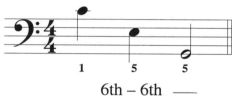

6th – 6th ——
or
4th – 4th ——

6th – 5th ——
or
3rd – 6th ——

4th – 5th ——
or
5th – 6th ——

5th – 4th ——
or
4th – 6th ——

Extra Credit: Play the above examples on the piano for 5 extra points each.

Perfect score: 50   **Your Score:** _____

With extra credit: 100

60

21

Baker's Blues

Words by Crystal Bowman

This StoryRhyme uses the intervals you have learned (2nd, 3rd, 4th, 5th and 6th).
Write the correct note to complete the interval on the staff. Then name both notes in the blanks.
Have fun reading the *StoryRhyme!*

down a 2nd   down a 5th   down a 6th

I tri __ __ to __ ak __ some __ ooki __ s

but I left them in too long.

down a 2nd   up a 5th   up a 6th   down a 3rd

I tri __ __ to b __ k __ a cho __ ol __ te __ __ ke

but everything went wrong.

up a 3rd

I tried to bake a __ h __ rry pie, but it sure tasted sour.

up a 2nd   up a 2nd   up a 4th

I __ or __ ot the su __ __ r and instead I __ __ ded flour!

down a 2nd   down a 4th   up a 4th

I tri __ __ to m __ k __ some __ rowni __ s

down a 2nd

but I dropp __ __ them on the floor.

up a 6th   up a 4th   down a 5th

I think I'll stop this __ akin __ __ n __ start h __ __ ding for the store!

(Your teacher may ask you to play the notes in the *StoryRhyme* on the piano.)

Sightreading Bonanza!

Sightread these musical examples that use **2nds**, **3rds**, **4ths**, **5ths** and **6ths**!
Set a slow, steady beat of one full measure before you begin. Always keep your eyes moving ahead!
Your teacher will keep a record of your progress with "Fabulous Notes" (correct notes) and
"Frightful Notes" (incorrect notes).

Each week try for an improved sightreading score!

Perfect score: 50

Date: **Score:**

_____ (1st week)   _____ Fabulous Notes   _____ Frightful Notes

_____ (2nd week)   _____ Fabulous Notes   _____ Frightful Notes

_____ (3rd week)   _____ Fabulous Notes   _____ Frightful Notes

Lesson 8   The Sharp

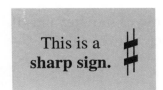

This is a
sharp sign. ♯

A *sharp* means to play the very next key to the right (up a half step).
A sharp is always a black key except for E♯ and B♯.

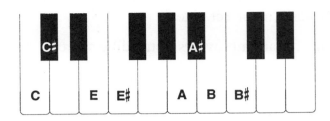

Play each key named on this keyboard saying its name aloud.

A sharp can be written on a line ♯ or in a space ♯.

Draw a sharp *in front of* each space note. Notice the sharp goes inside the space ♯.
Then name each note in the blank.

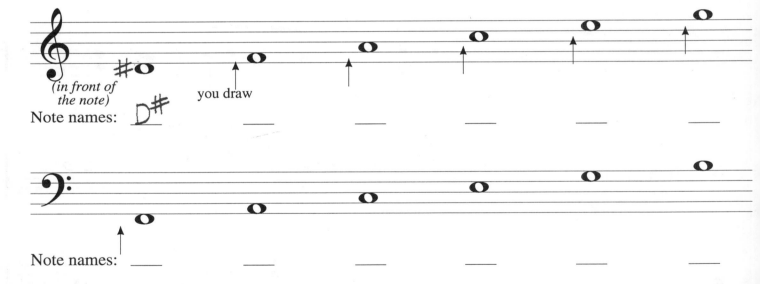

*(in front of
the note)*
you draw

Note names: D♯   ____   ____   ____   ____   ____

Note names: ____   ____   ____   ____   ____

Now play all the sharped notes above on the piano.

Guide notes

Draw a sharp *in front of* each of the
guide notes shown.

Then play each one on the piano,
saying the letter names aloud.

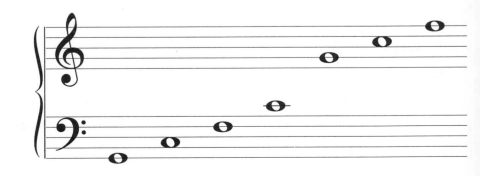

Draw a sharp in front of each note marked with an arrow.
Then write the name of each note in the blank.

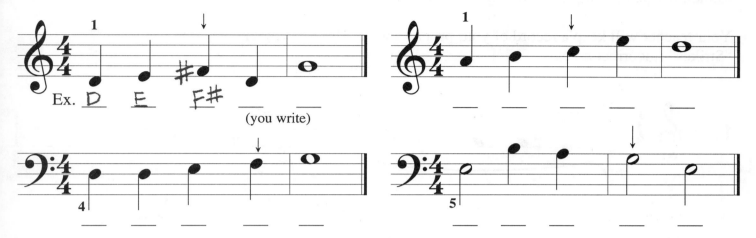

(you write)

Play each example above on the piano.

A sharp lasts for the whole measure, but not after the barline.
In a new measure, the sharp must be written again.

still F♯

The sharp must be written again.
(new measure)

Write in the letter names of each note below.
Be sure to include the sharp sign when naming the note.

(Your teacher may ask you to play the examples above on the piano.)

Sightreading Bonanza!

Sightread these musical examples that use sharps.

Remember that a sharp lasts through the entire measure.

Your teacher will keep a record of your progress with "Hits" (correct notes) and "Strikes" (incorrect notes).

Perfect score: 50

Date:

_____ (1st week)

_____ (2nd week)

_____ (3rd week)

Score:

_____ Hits   _____ Strikes

_____ Hits   _____ Strikes

_____ Hits   _____ Strikes

The Flat

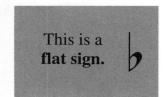
This is a **flat sign.**

A *flat* means to play the very next key to the left (down a half step).
A *flat* is always a black key except for C♭ and F♭.

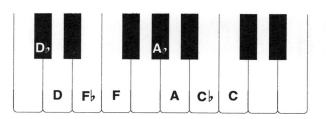

Play each key named on this keyboard saying its name aloud.

A flat can be written on a line or in a space.

Draw a flat *in front of* each line note. Notice the line goes through the middle of the flat.
Then name each note in the blank.

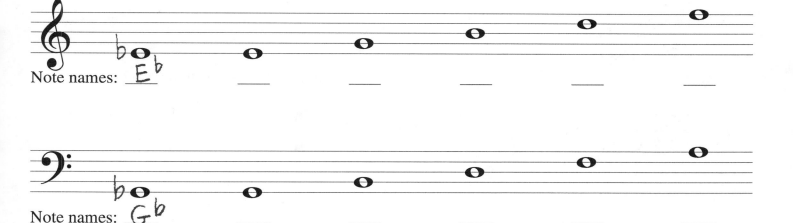

Note names: E♭ ___ ___ ___ ___ ___

Note names: G♭ ___ ___ ___ ___ ___

Now play all the flatted notes above on the piano.

Draw a flat *in front of* each space note below.
Name each note in the blank. Then play each example on the keyboard.

___   ___   ___   ___

The Flats Meet the Sharps

Give the flat name and sharp name for each black key marked with an X.
Then write both the sharp and flat notes on the staffs to the right.

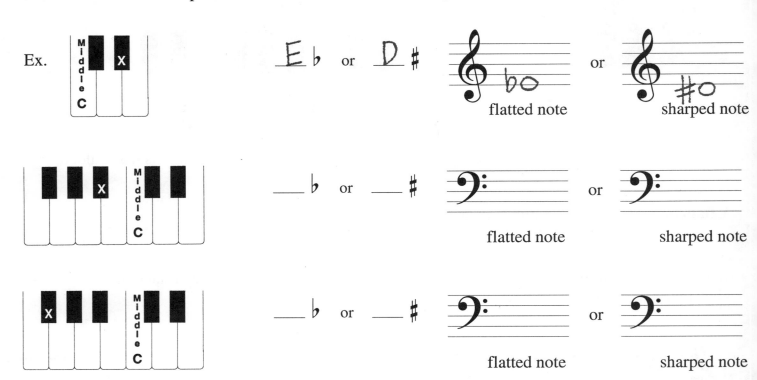

Ex.   E♭ or D♯

flatted note   sharped note

___ ♭ or ___ ♯

flatted note   sharped note

___ ♭ or ___ ♯

flatted note   sharped note

Circle the correct letter names for each example below. Then play the music on the piano.

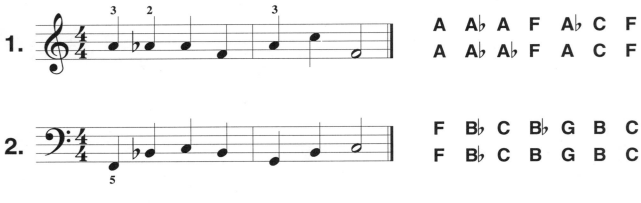

1.
A A♭ A F A♭ C F
A A♭ A♭ F A C F

2.
F B♭ C B♭ G B C
F B♭ C B G B C

The following examples have both sharps and flats!

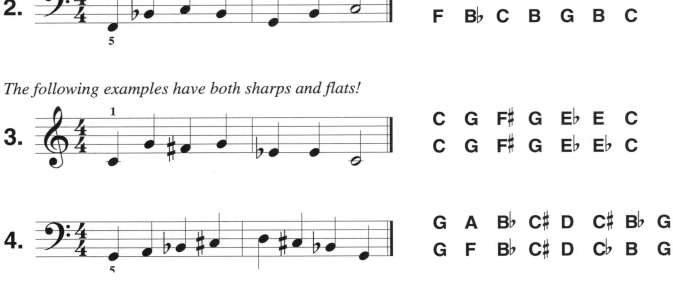

3.
C G F♯ G E♭ E C
C G F♯ G E♭ E♭ C

4.
G A B♭ C♯ D C♯ B♭ G
G F B♭ C♯ D C♭ B G

Sightreading Bonanza!

Sightread these musical examples that use flats.

Remember that a flat lasts through the entire measure.

Your teacher will keep a record of your progress with "Super Notes" (correct notes) and "Silly Notes" (incorrect notes).

Perfect score: 50

Date: **Score:**

_____ (1st week)   _____ **Super Botes**   _____ **Silly Notes**

_____ (2nd week)   _____ **Super Notes**   _____ **Silly Notes**

_____ (3rd week)   _____ **Super Notes**   _____ **Silly Notes**

Lesson 10 — The Natural

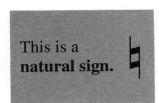

This is a **natural sign.**

A *natural* sign ♮ cancels a sharp or flat.
A natural sign always indicates a white key.

Ex.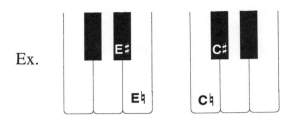

A natural can be written on a line ♮ or in a space ♮.

Trace the naturals below using these two steps. First, draw the shape of an "L",

then draw the shape of a "7". Notice a box is formed. ♮ ← box

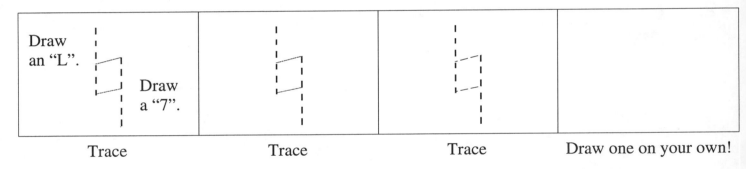

| Draw an "L". Draw a "7". | | | |
| Trace | Trace | Trace | Draw one on your own! |

Trace the naturals on the staffs below. Write the letter name of each in the blank.

Ex. E♮

Sharps, Flats, and Naturals!

Name each example below with the correct letter name and symbol. Notice the clef sign!

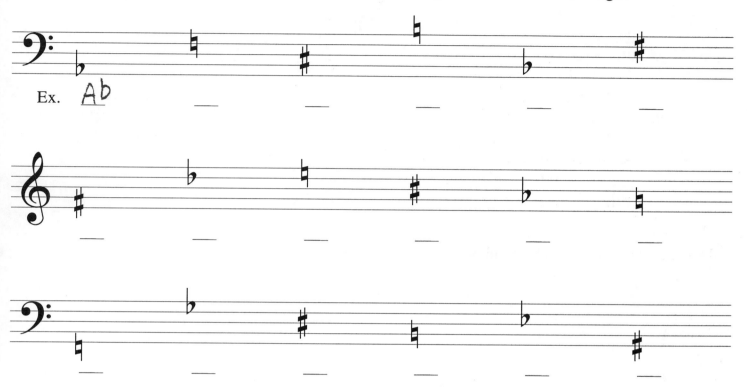

Ex. A♭

Name each note below. Then sightread the examples on the piano.

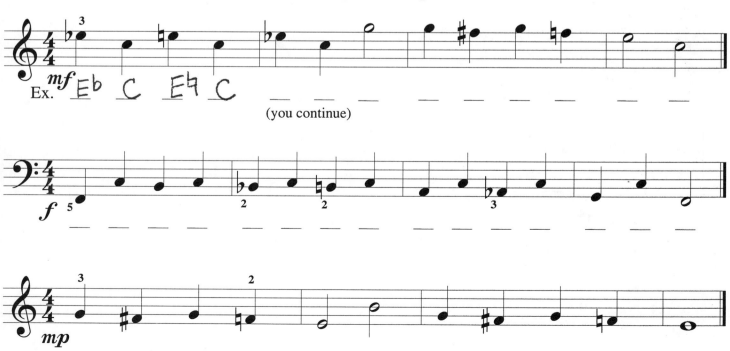

Ex. *mf* E♭ C E♮ C

(you continue)

Final Review

The End of the Rainbow

Write the correct notes to complete the rainbow below. Use whole notes.
See if you can correctly land at the pot of gold at the end of the rainbow!

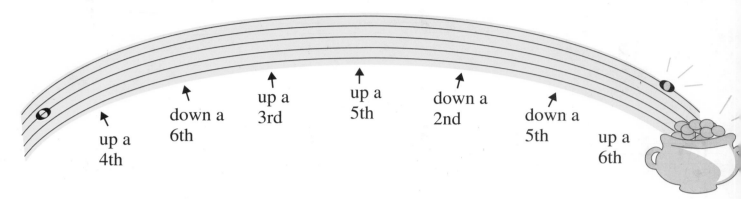

Name each guide note and symbol correctly. Then play them on the piano using any finger.

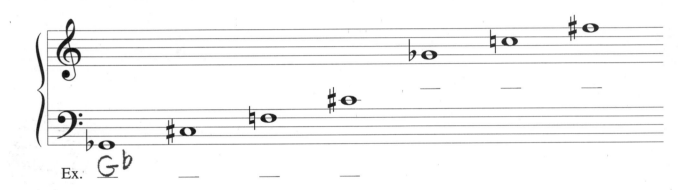

Ex. G♭

Name each space note below.

Name each line note below.

Perfect score: 50

_____ **Sweet Notes**   _____ **Sour Notes**